GENEROSITY

RUBENS RUBA

DEDICATION

This book is dedicated to the most gracious Lord and
Savior Jesus Christ and to the most gracious woman I
know on earth – my wife, Beth

TABLE OF CONTENTS

INTRODUCTION

Laura and Roger Griffiths thought that it was the opportunity of a lifetime because they had just won a 2.7 million dollars 2005 payoff lottery. Up to that point, their marriage was peaceful. They decided to buy whatever they wanted with all that money. She bought a beautiful home and he bought the Porsche that he wanted. But six years after that win, they "divorced." Their fourteen-year marriage was over and they had run through every penny of their fortune.

The Griffiths payout became their undoing. The sad part of this story is that they planned on living a great life with all that money. They planned on investing some of it. They planned on doing some good with most of it. But all that went unrealized.

In many ways, we are like this young couple when it comes to money. In our fallen state, our natural inclination, and often our practice, is to spend everything we have on ourselves. And if we don't have money of our own, we will use credit cards to extend our spending power beyond our ability.

Most people don't make the mistake that this couple made. But regardless of how we spend it, we think our money is exactly that: ours. Without a guide or advisor, we may get to the end of our life and look back and wonder what we did with all that we had.

From cover to cover, the Bible is replete with examples on the issue of material wealth.

- Lot's and Abraham's herdsman quarreled because of an abundance of possessions.
- Esau "sold" his birthright for a mere bowl of stew.
- Joseph's brothers spared his life in order to gain a little profit.
- Moses disavowed great wealth to do what God called him to do.
- The Israelites plundered their Egyptian masters then used that wealth to make a false god in the wilderness.
- Ruth and Naomi had not a penny to their

names, but found favor from God through a
wealthy man named Boaz.

- David went from rags to riches, while
  Solomon went from wealth to utter despair.
- The Pharisees lived in wealth, while the
  Savior had no place to lay his head.
- Anannias and Sapphira lied and died over
  giving their money to the church, while the
  Macedonians gave until it hurt.

While we may or may not feel we have enough
money to live on today, God promises that one day
we will walk with solid gold under our feet.

What we do with our money matters.

Our perspective on money, possessions, and how we
handle them, lies at the very heart of the Christian
life. The Bible dramatically demonstrates that how
we view our money and possessions is of utmost
importance. What we do with them will influence
eternity.

Jesus told his disciples a story in Luke, *"There was a
rich man whose manager was accused of wasting his
possessions. ² So he called him in and asked him, 'What is
this I hear about you? Give an account of your
management, because you cannot be manager any longer"*

(Luke 16:1-2). This parable shows that God, who is infinitely rich and owns all things, has assigned us management responsibilities over his resources.

The danger is to see money as a toy to play rather than a tool to impact eternity. It is then that our vision becomes short sighted. We become wasteful and we tend to live rather recklessly. That is when we need to think differently about our "things" and that is what this book is about.

As Martin Luther put it, *"There are three conversions necessary in the Christian life: the conversion of the heart, the mind and the purse."*

What I would like to do in this book is to take you through how God taught mankind to be giving and generous. As you can see in the example above, it doesn't come naturally. It must be Spirit-led and, in many ways, taught.

Let's see through various examples in God's Word how he taught us how to be generous givers. For that is his ultimate goal.

Chapter 1

SETTLING ON OWNERSHIP

*H*aving a Biblical world-view of money is often very difficult because it clashes with the way we grow up in our society. A *biblical worldview* says God owns my money, and therefore, I'm a steward of it. A *cultural worldview* says my money is mine, and I can do whatever I want with it.

I remember when my kids were still living under my roof and wanted to learn how to drive a car. They bugged us to get their license for a couple of years and finally we gave in. We could sense their newfound feeling of freedom and independence when we decided to buy another car because they had to get to an after school job, but of course, it came with a price. It always does. Liz and Abi had to be at our beck and call in order to run errands for us at our convenience. The reason was that it was still our vehicle and they were still living under our roof. They could use it, and they had a certain amount of responsibility to take care of it, but the car was ours.

The key issue was ownership. It was still Mom and Dad's car. They could use it with our permission. I know it got under their skin at times, but they learned to understand the definitions of ownership and responsibility.

A biblical world view understands that God is the owner of everything that we have, and that we are merely managers (stewards) of His resources. Yes, we have our homes, cars, boats, vacation homes and toys, but it all belongs to him and we need to keep that in mind.

Keeping this fact in perspective helps transform every financial decision we make. I often say that every financial decision is a spiritual decision.

Who is the Owner?

Let's take a look at what the Bible has to say about who owns our money. As you read the following verses, underline everything God owns. For everything comes from him.

[14] *But who am I, and who are my people, that we should be*

able to give as generously as this? Everything comes from you, and we have given you only what comes from your hand.

1 Chronicles 29:14

I have no need of a bull from your stall or of goats from your pens, [10] for every animal of the forest is mine, and the cattle on a thousand hills. [11] I know every bird in the mountains, and the insects in the fields are mine [12] If I were hungry I would not tell you, for the world is mine, and all that is in it.

Psalm 50:9-12

The earth is the LORD's, and everything in it, the world, and all who live in it.

Psalm 24:1

The Problem

As you can see in these passages, Scripture is very clear about who owns the earth and all the rest of creation. The problem most of us have isn't with acknowledging that God owns the earth; it's acknowledging that God owns our personal stuff.

For some reason it is much easier to think of the trees and the animals belonging to God, but when God's ownership extends to our possessions, we find it much harder to believe God owns it all. However, Scripture is very clear that everything on the earth is the Lord's, including all our personal possessions.

Dangers Of Not Believing This Truth

Let's briefly look at some of the dangers of not believing this truth.

In the following passage draw a box around everything God did for the Israelites. Then circle everything the Israelites did for themselves.

God Owns it All

[10] When you have eaten and are satisfied, praise the Lord your God for the good land he has given you. [11] Be careful that you do not forget the Lord your God, failing to observe his commands, his laws and his decrees that I am giving you this day. [12] Otherwise, when you eat and are satisfied, when you build fine houses and settle down, [13] and when your herds and flocks grow large and your silver and gold increase and all you have is multiplied, [14] then your heart will become proud and you will forget the Lord your God, who brought you out of Egypt, out of the land of slavery. [15] He led you through the vast and dreadful wilderness, that thirsty and waterless land, with its venomous snakes and scorpions. He brought you water out of hard rock. [16] He gave you manna to eat in

the wilderness, something your ancestors had never known, to humble and test you so that in the end it might go well with you. ¹⁷ You may say to yourself, "My power and the strength of my hands have produced this wealth for me." ¹⁸ But remember the Lord your God, for it is he who gives you the ability to produce wealth, and so confirms his covenant, which he swore to your ancestors, as it is today. ¹⁹ If you ever forget the Lord your God and follow other gods and worship and bow down to them, I testify against you today that you will surely be destroyed.²⁰ Like the nations the Lord destroyed before you, so you will be destroyed for not obeying the Lord your God.
Deuteronomy 8:10-20

Ok. You didn't have to circle too many things that they did for themselves, did you? Did you notice how the Israelites were dependent on God? This attitude that the Israelites had with forgetting all that God did for them is so prevalent in our lives.

In fact, when I look at this passage, I see three dangerous steps that can happen through prosperity that we need to be aware.

The first attitude that can creep into our lives when we see blessing and prosperity is *pride*. In Verse 14, Moses talks about how pride causes us to forget about God. In the illustration given above, the nation of Israel would forget how God had worked in their lives in the past by taking them out of slavery and leading them through the wilderness. They would forget about the dangerous snakes and scorpions that they were protected from. In the same way, as prosperity comes into our lives and we begin to become "comfortable," we forget.

- We forget our sinful past.
- We forget how God saved us and blessed us.
- We forget the grace of God and we begin to, as one writer put it, "read our press clippings and actually believe them."

The second danger in prosperity is *self-sufficiency* rather than dependence on the Lord. In Verse 17, we find the writer stating, *"My power and the strength of my hands have produced this wealth for me."* Not too long ago, our church was looking for some property to relocate our facility and we took a tour of a huge house with acreage. It was rather sad to learn that the owners had built up a huge business, but because of illegal dealings were in jail. As we toured, pictures of their beautiful family were still on the walls and their home office. This beautiful home that was sitting on top of this huge property on a hill was not dedicated to the Lord. It reminded me that self-sufficiency can never end well.

The third danger seen in this passage is *forgetting God and following idols*. In Verses 19 and 20 give a pretty grim picture.

If you ever forget the Lord your God and follow other gods and worship and bow down to them, I testify against you today that you will surely be destroyed.[20] *Like the nations the Lord destroyed before you, so you will be destroyed for not obeying the Lord your God*
Deuteronomy 8:19-20

Tremendous temptation and danger threaten us when we fall into the trap of believing we're responsible for our own success. The world tells us we can be anything we want to be. This is a complete lie.

Rather, we can be anything God created us to be. We have a responsibility to cultivate the gifts, resources, and abilities we've been given to the very best of our abilities, but we can't forget the source of those gifts, resources, or abilities.

I'm 5 feet 9 inches tall with a minimal vertical leap and rather slow. I couldn't have been a professional basketball player, even in my prime, no matter how hard I worked. God didn't create me that way. However, I was gifted in other ways. I view these gifts as coming from the Lord, and I believe it's my responsibility to use them to my fullest.

If you're willing to be 100 percent honest with yourself, you'll realize that the reason you're successful are the skills you were born with and the circumstances in which you were raised. It is because God gave them to you.

We received all these things by *God's sovereign grace.*

Thereby, we recognize the truth that God is the owner of all our resources and we are stewards and not owners. A steward is simply a manager for someone else.

My personal, long-standing definition of stewardship is:

The use of God-given gifts and resources—such as time, talent, treasure, influence, and relationships—for the accomplishment of God-given goals and objectives

This is what Christ wanted from us. He wanted us to turn over ownership of our lives to him.

You then have two choices.

You can live your life as if Christ is not at all the owner, or you can live your life as if God is the owner and you are but a steward (manager) of everything that God has in your care. It is your choice.

I'm a very practical person. I like steps. So let me end with a couple of areas to help you start in this area of turning your life over from being the owner to the manager of your "stuff."

1. *Ownership requires personal faith in Christ.*

Have you ever placed your faith in Jesus as your Lord and Savior of your life? This can be done by an act of faith in Christ by repenting from your sin and asking Him to be your Savior. In John 20:31 we read, *"But these are written that you may believe that Jesus is the Messiah, the Son of God, and that by believing you may have life in his name."*

If you don't know the type of words you might use, here is a sample prayer that you might express to God. But let me emphasize that it's not the words, but what is in your heart's desire that will give you the assurance of your salvation and forgiveness of sin.

Lord Jesus, I know that I am a sinner and I cannot save myself. My good works cannot save me. My church going cannot save me. But today, I turn over the ownership of my life to you. I repent from my sins and to the best of my ability I place my faith in you. In Jesus Name I pray.
Amen.

Entering a relationship with Christ is critical to surrendering everything in a person's life. If you recognize Jesus Christ as your Lord and Savior, then the first requirement from such a person is obedience. The obedience is given to Jesus Christ because of the authority that was granted to Him. Jesus said as He departed for his throne in glory, *"All authority in Heaven and on earth has been given to me"* (Matthew 28:18). When you place your faith in Jesus, you are saying, "Jesus, you call the shots in my life from this day forward!" But it doesn't stop there. There is still a struggle for independence and ownership. That's why a second truth is also important to know.

2. Ownership is a day to day experience of yielding ourselves to the Holy Spirit.

If I say to God in my daily prayer, "Oh Lord, I yield myself to You," what I mean is that based on the fact that I belong to him, I now live my life in obedience to Jesus. "I'm no longer my owner, my master, or my shepherd. For you are my Owner, Master, Shepherd, Father, and lasting pleasure. I renounce finding all of that is in me. I look for it now in you, because I am completely yours." That means that, day to day I look to him for the power to live the Christian life.

The Divine Purchase

In theological circles, we call this "The Divine Purchase." In 1 Corinthians 6, we read of this purchase. *"Do you not know that your body is a temple of the Holy Spirit within you, whom you have from God? You are not your own, for you were bought with a price. So glorify God in your body"* (1 Corinthians 6:9).

That's a fact. God did that. God has purchased a people for himself. They are not their own. They belong to God. That is, they exist to glorify and enjoy God forever. Their sins are forgiven. Their guilt is taken away. Their rebellion is overcome. What they say is, "I'm happy about that. I agree with that. I give myself freely and joyfully to the one who has purchased me."

Settling on ownership is bringing yourself into alignment with what God has already achieved for you. *Giving yourself to God* means longing for him to completely possess, rule, satisfy, and use you for his purposes.

One way of expressing this is found in Romans chapter 12 verse 1, where Paul says, *"I appeal to you therefore, brothers, by the mercies of God, **to present your bodies** as a living sacrifice, holy and acceptable to God, which is your spiritual [**service of**] worship."* "I give myself to God" means:

• I receive the mercies,

• I present my body as a living sacrifice.

• It is as an act of worship.

• I long for God to completely possess me, rule me, satisfy me, use me for His purposes.

The Human Response

In Romans 16:13 it says, *"Do not present your members"* — your mind, or your arms and legs, tongue and so on — *"to sin as instruments for unrighteousness, but present yourselves to God as those who have been brought from death to life, and your members to God as instruments for righteousness."*

When we read those words and want to obey it, we say, "I present to you, O God, myself, my memory, my arms, my legs, my hands, my eyes, my tongue, so that you may possess them as your own, and accomplish your good and holy purposes through the use of myself, my body, my soul as instruments of righteousness. I give myself to you."

There's a beautiful story in 2 Corinthians about how the Macedonians did this. It says, *"They gave themselves first of all to the Lord, and then by the will of God also to us* (2 Corinthians 8:4-5). In other words, their commitment to the Lord brought out a selfless monetary gift to the church in Jerusalem.

Then we have the great example of Jesus. From the cross, Jesus called out with a loud voice *"'Father, into your hands I commit my spirit!' And having said this he breathed his last"*(Luke 23:46). *"Into your hands I commit my spirit"* is another way of saying I give myself to you.

It's no surprise, that when the early Christians were going to describe their own suffering and death they chose some of the same words. For instance in 1 Peter 4:19 we read: *"So then, those who suffer according to God's will should commit themselves to their faithful Creator and continue to do good."*

Entrusting your soul to a faithful Creator means, "I give myself to you. God, you're faithful. You're powerful. You're my Creator. I belong to you. You made me. Take care of me now.

Ownership – Creation and Redemption

In the Scriptures, there are two reasons of why God is presented as the owner of our lives. First, is the fact that we are created in his image. Therefore, he is the owner (1 Peter 4:19). But the second reason goes deeper and even more personal. He is the owner of our lives because He is our redeemer.

I think the key for all of us when it comes to the area of ownership is not just in the area of creation. But we must settle it in our minds and in our hearts whether we believe we have been purchased by God through Christ or not.

Do we believe that we are not our own? Do we believe that we are utterly dependent on God for our life, our choices, our provision, our protection, our satisfaction, our meaning, and our hope of eternal joy? If in fact God has purchased us for this, then the words I give myself to you, means, "Yes, yes, yes."

Yes, to your purchase of me. I am thrilled to be utterly yours, bought with the price of your Son in this way. I renounce, therefore, all self-reliance, all self-exaltation. I give myself utterly to you for your use forever.

LIFE APPLICATION

1. Read Isaiah 48:17-19. What blessings would you lose by going your own way and failing to recognize God's ownership?
2. How much of your life are you willing for God to control? How much of it does he control?
3. Is there something in your life that you have not surrendered to the control of your heavenly Father? What is it, and how will you now deal with it?
4. What do you think God will do with your life if you surrender it all to him?

Chapter 2

SIGNIFICANCE LEADS TO GENEROSITY

J realized that as a Pastor I was failing. I was preaching sermons and trying to persuade people about the power of tithing and giving to the church, but somehow I was missing the mark. For the past thirty years I've been preaching to congregations on the subject, as well as leading small group meetings, yet, it seemed that I just couldn't get through to them.

I finally realized why this was the case. I couldn't explain to them why it was *so important* for them to give. That's why this book is so critical for me. It's led me back to reflect on generosity because it's not about tithing or giving to the church which is the issue. It really comes down to the heart of generosity. That's the why.

To put it succinctly, I've come to the conclusion that generosity is not in our DNA. I know that some people are more prone to give than others. But biblical generosity as God defines is hard to live out. In fact, this book will only touch a small section of God's intention on the subject.

For the majority of us, generosity is not something we wake up with each day thinking about. It's not in our DNA. If there's any doubt about that it, just go to a small child and try to take away a "toy" and you will hear the words: MINE. There is in every one of us a selfish nature that craves narcissism to a certain extent.

So it's not in our DNA to be generous, but why is that so important? Well, I'm at the point in my life that I am thinking about what it means to be leave a legacy. On top of that, my personality trait is to be a very goal setting person. I like to get things accomplished. Therefore, I'm wrestling with being content and sometimes even with gratitude of where I am in life. And all that leaves me empty at times.

Significance Through Things

Recently, I heard of a story of a person who really lived his life for the acquisition of things. I'm sure he didn't start out that to do that. He has expensive cars in his driveway, a gorgeous home, and he goes on multiple expensive vacations, golfs two to three times a week, but to hear him talk about his family life and their future, he is rather fatalistic. Things do not give meaning.

Significance and Generosity

Robert McGee wrote a book entitled *A Search for Significance,* and I stumbled into some thoughts from him that I thought were very beneficial. Robert talked about how everyone desires a life of *significance.* Using a baseball metaphor, he said that we run the bases wrong. We seek to achieve significance by chasing success at the cost of the people around us and end up with no *self-respect.*

Certainly, there are a lot of leaders with success in politics, business and even in religion who have fallen. They spend years seeking to repair the damage done by their stupid pursuit of success at the cost of their own character.

But here is my epiphany. A life of significance can only be attained through *generosity.* Booker T. Washington, the great 19th century educator and founder of Tuskegee University in Alabama noted, "Those are happiest who do the most for others."

Let me explain: *significance is at the core of every human life*. Whether you are a Christian or Non-Christian, it really doesn't matter. God placed it there. In Ecclesiastes 3:11 the Bible tells us, *"He has made everything beautiful in its time. He has also set eternity in the human heart; yet no one can fathom what God has done from beginning to end (Ecclesiastes 3:11)*. First, this verse tells us that we are only here for a temporary time. No matter how many times we hit the gym, there is an appointed time for us to die. But second, this verse reminds us of an innate desire to be a part of something that lasts beyond our lifetime.

I can only attain significance by surrendering my life to Jesus Christ who gives me that innate desire. We call it the "greater cause." This is where men and women have sought to build bridges, paint beautiful paintings, build great edifices, dedicate museums and libraries.

From the Biblical perspective, you and I can only attain true, full and deep significance when we first surrender our life to Jesus Christ.

To continue to use the baseball analogy, I begin to run the bases the right way and that's when I surrender to the Lordship of Christ. That's when I start to love others in community. Jesus said it this way:

A new command I give you: Love one another. As I have loved you, so you must love one another. [35] By this everyone will know that you are my disciples, if you love one another" (John13:34-35)

Great love is marked by generosity. As I love others, I will also find myself being generous to other people. And that will lead to a life of significance. To sum it up, we get significance by surrendering our lives to Christ, and loving others in community and generosity.

An Example

As I pondered this chapter, I realized that Jesus was the greatest example describing my thoughts. He was completely surrendered to the Will of the Father even to the very end of his life. Yet, throughout his life, he was the most generous.

Think about it.

- He would stay late into the night as people were bringing the sick, the lame, the deaf and the blind to Him.
- He defended the adulterous woman who was caught in sin and was about to be stoned.

- He noticed Zaccheus up in a tree and dined with him.
- In fact, John 21:25 sums up Jesus' generous life in this way:

Jesus did many other things as well. If every one of them were written down, I suppose that even the whole world would not have room for the books that would be written
John 20:25

What is the goal of a life of generosity? For each us it is individual joy. How do I know that? Because in Hebrews 12:2 it says this about our Lord. The Lord set his sights on joy.

For the joy set before him he endured the cross, scorning its shame, and sat down at the right hand of the throne of God (Hebrews 12:2).

It's interesting that in this passage, the writer of Hebrews tells us to *consider Him* as we look at our lives. Each of us is to consider "Christ" as our example for generosity.

- He was self-less
- He was giving
- He was totally sacrificial

- He was all in when it came to racially redeeming you and me.
- His generosity level was the highest.

Let me go back to my initial thought.

Generosity is not natural to us and that's why I believe God has to teach what it means to be a generous people. Because, it is through generosity that significance is attained. And God wants us to feel significance.

Throughout history, He has used a variety of methods and tools to teach His people how to be generous and in this book we will be discussing some of these such as tithing, giving to the poor, and even grace giving.

For now, understand that generosity is something all of us desire and yet struggle. It is not a natural by-product. Pray that God will increase this gracious spirit in your life as you continue reading.

LIFE APPLICATION

1. Before reading this chapter, how would you have defined generosity?
2. What do people usually pursue in their search for significance? Do you agree that "a life of significance leads to a life of generosity?"
3. Generosity is difficult to discuss and hard to define. It seems that it is only the rich who can deal with this issue. What questions do you have about generosity?

Chapter 3

IT'S REALLY BRILLIANT TO BE GENEROUS

I'm not really sure where I came up with the idea but until I was in my 20's, I thought that generosity was for the rich or the much spiritual person. I was safe since I felt I wasn't in either category.

I wasn't selfish, but generosity wasn't the first thing on my mind. They weren't values to be embraced and sought after. In my mind, generosity required a lot of things I didn't have like a big bank account and even a greater heart for God. I came from a middle class home where Mom and Dad struggled to make ends meet and paying for college was tough.

Fast forward, and in my first year after college graduation, I accepted a part-time position as a youth pastor at a small church in Philadelphia. It was there

I met Dr. Cook. He was a very stately man who I later found out was very well off financially and who made his money in the dairy business. But his heart wasn't just with cows, it really was with people.

Being in a city church, as a Youth Pastor, I would go out and play basketball in the local playground, and before long I had befriended some really good basketball players. I got the idea that we could join the local Christian basketball league of churches and "clean up." These kids were phenomenal basketball players. The only problem was that the league required uniforms and these teens were mostly from the lower economic level. Dr. Cook heard about it and the next day came into my office and handed me a check for $500 in order to buy brand new uniforms and basketballs. I tried to tell him that I wasn't sure if these kids would stay with the team or if they would even come to church, but he said, "It's not about the team or the church, it's about showing the love of God to them. They need to feel special."

Dr. Cook and I became friends throughout a number of years. In fact, I owe him a whole lot. He eventually was instrumental in paying for my entire Master of Divinity education program when I really didn't have the money to continue studying. But I'm sure that he didn't just do it with me. In fact, years later I found out that a number of people were affected by his generosity in the Lord's work.

I'm sure you see the spiritual correlation by now. This is a pretty powerful picture of our relationship with God and the way we manage his resources. Dr. Cook came into my office and gave me a check for $500 and said, *"Manage my resources,"* and I then had the responsibility to act on behalf of his interest for those high school players.

I may not have the income level of a Dr. Cook, but God has given us great resources. And I do believe that God has given us the opportunity to act in his interests as we represent him to the world.

Generosity Is A Brilliant Way To Live

I hope that you noticed that there was no obligation between Dr. Cook and me. There was no sacrificial lambs slaughtered or guilt trips. There were no letters sent, but merely a need shared that a group of kids who need Jesus and love playing basketball needed uniforms. That's God's design for the way we give and express generosity. It's meant to be joyful and fulfilling. It isn't rooted in guilt or self-righteousness.

In Hebrews, the word "generosity" means to saturate with water, or a symbol of life. It means to overflow in a way that it brings life to people. In the Greek, it means, ready to distribute. It also means, available to give time, talent and treasure.

When you put these two definitions together, you get a dramatic picture of a life overflowing with care and concern for others. *Isn't generosity a brilliant way to live?*

It isn't supposed to be a sacrificial, "pulling your teeth" type of picture for the super-spiritual. I would say it this way that,"*saving and spending carefully is a wise way to live, but giving generously is brilliant.*" Both practically and spiritually, it's one of the best ways to live your life no matter what your income level may be.

Generosity Does Work

When people are generous and gracious they radiate joy and happiness. There's something attractive about those who have a sense of kindness and do nice things. As I write this chapter, a request came from a church member whose lawn needed to be mowed. Usually, when our church receives these types of requests, we try to immediately send out an email. Within only a few minutes the request was taken care by a group of young adults from our ministry. It just brings a smile when I think of young people sharing their time and efforts.

Four Reasons Why It is Brilliant To Live A Generous Life

First, *generosity enriches our lives.* Jesus said, *"It is more blessed to give than to receive"* (Acts 20:35). You will be happier. Proverbs 11:24 states the same idea: *"One person gives freely, yet gains even more; another withholds unduly, but comes to poverty."* There is a general principle that generosity changes our lives. People who give generously feel good about it and find themselves blessed in ways they never expected. Great things happen in them, and great things happen to those around them. It's the ultimate win-win situation. When Dr. Cook paid for my education, that changed my life. It opened the opportunity for me to become a Senior Pastor. I can't imagine not having that opportunity.

Second, *generosity unites us with other people.* It just seems that wherever your money goes, your heart follows. If you want to be connected, then generosity does that. When people are generous and gracious, they exude love and happiness. Generous people create positive feelings in their relationships. My wife, Beth who is our church administrator, is really good at this. People who are hurting come into our church office all the time needing food and money. There's an application process that they go through and usually we provide a local food gift card to help them. I'm always amazed how Beth is able to learn their "story" in the process. Usually it's a pretty hard life story that they share. Many are down to their last few dollars and they could be evicted from their homes. But usually by the end of the hour they are giving Beth a hug and so thankful for the gift.

Third, *generosity helps us commit to what matters the most in life.* Jesus talks in Matthew 6 about two treasures and two masters. He says, *"Do not store up for yourselves treasures on earth, where moths and vermin destroy, and where thieves break in and steal.* [20] *But store up for yourselves treasures in heaven, where moths and vermin do not destroy, and where thieves do not break in and steal* [Matthew 6:19-20). The timeless principle that Jesus gives is this: [21] *For where your treasure is, there your heart will be also* (Matthew 6:21).

In Matthew 6, he is not saying that it's wrong to save. The *store up for yourselves* is in reference to greed, hoarding and false security. But, what's the reason? What is Jesus' motivation? It's a bad investment! It will not last. It is not secure. It is dangerous and it can't last in the long run.

Spiritually, generosity protects us from shortsighted, bad investments of our time, our talent, and our treasure and creates long-term wealth. Jesus is saying in Matthew 6, that everything you do is an investment. You are always pouring your time, talent, and treasure into something. And whatever you're pouring into, that's where your heart is. So don't store up treasure for yourselves that which will not deliver in the long run. Fame, success, and money is all temporal.

But notice that Jesus then goes on and says, *"Store up treasures _for yourselves_ in heaven."* Please notice that I underlined the words *"for yourselves."* We always get the idea that stewardship is giving something up almost as a martyr. But you gain when you give as God desires. If you believe that there is a Heaven then you believe then there is a time of GREAT rewards. Smart people don't just invest for the now, they invest for the future.

Fourth, *generosity frees us up.* In Matthew 6, Jesus also talks about two masters. In verse 24, it says, *No one can serve two masters. Either you will hate the one and love the other, or you will be devoted to the one and despise the other. You cannot serve both God and money* (Matthew 6:24). Let me ask you a question: What is the opposite of God? Most of us would say, "Satan."

But that's not what Jesus said. Jesus said that there are two masters. He doesn't say that there is Yahweh and then there is Satan. But He says that there is *God and money – of course, energized by the enemy.* But where your time, energy, thoughts and even what drives your life is centered, God considers it the devotion of your *worship*.

According to Jesus, there is option A (God) or option B (Money). And the only way to break your heart free from money is to live a life of generosity.

I don't know where you are in this area of generosity. I don't know if you are reading this book with a lot of suspicion thinking that all this writer/Pastor is after is to get into your wallet.

But this book really is about a generous heart. It is more than giving to my church or any church. Because I've found that truly generous people are always looking for people and causes to give to. They are not tied to the 10% tithing rule. They are not satisfied with just giving a gift in the offering plate.

Generosity is a lifestyle.

For generosity is a lifestyle. But it has to be learned. And God knew that it is a hard lesson to teach and that's why he started to teach it in the Old Testament and continued to teach generosity into the New Testament. Because generosity doesn't come naturally. It is not part of our DNA and it must learned by the work of the Holy Spirit.

In the next few chapters, we're going to understand the place and importance of tithing in our lives. But again it goes beyond the ten percent.

I remember when I was a teenager giving one dollar to the Lord's work and then when I started a lawn cutting job I gave five dollars a week to the Lord's work and thought I was doing pretty good. But then I got around some really generous people who gave not only their tithe, but also gave above their tithe to other causes. They weren't rich. They were regular middle class people. But they were generous and they looked at opportunities to give.

Generosity is a great way to live.

There are so many benefits.

On a scale between 1 to 10, how generous are you?

LIFE APPLICATION

Review the four reasons it is brilliant to be generous and react to the following questions.

1. How does generosity enrich your life?
2. How has generosity connected you with others?
3. How has generosity helped you invest in life?
4. How does generosity free up your heart?

Chapter 4

GENEROSITY BEGINS WITH TITHING

*F*or some people, tithing has been a part of their growing up experience in the church for as long as they can remember. For others, tithing is looked upon as a practice that is no longer to be applicable. They think that anyone who is giving the minimum of ten percent is in bondage to legalism. In fact, some even consider the teaching of it to be a cancer in churches. It is a manipulation tool by dishonest leaders used to fund their pet projects and excessive lifestyles.

Of course, there are those types of leaders, but the problem is with them, and not with tithing. I am bewildered by these extremes, and I do not align myself with either legalism, or with dishonest gain.

I specifically address tithing here not to promote

legalism, and not because I don't distinguish between the Old and New Testament covenants. I do it simply because it is where God began with his children in teaching them. Randy Alcorn calls tithing the *training wheels of giving.* I like that! I think that generosity does not come naturally to human beings. I think that we are, for the most part, self-centered. We need to be re-configured when it comes to giving, and tithing is one way to do that.

I'm not saying that we are completely selfish, but we have the tendency, for the most part, to focus on our inner circle of relationships such as our family members or our closest friends. The problem is that we get stuck there and God wants that circle to grow beyond it.

One of the ways that God has taught his children to expand that circle of concern is through tithing. At this point, please try to put aside some of your misconceptions about tithing and see what God wants to accomplish through it.

Definition of Tithing

Let's get something straight. The definition of tithing is ten percent. I've had people say to me that they are going to *tithe* 5%. Unfortunately you can't tithe 5% because the word *tithe* means 10%. Biblically, *tithing meant that we returned to the Lord the first tenth of His income before taxes and expenses.* The Jewish believer of the Old Testament would take from animals, produce and grain the first which was produced and bring that to his God. He understood that it belonged to the Lord.

Let's unpack the Old Testament principle of *tithing* and understand why God instituted this teaching tool.

Tithing Did Not Start Under The Law

First, understand that tithing did not start under the law. In fact, the entire concept of putting God first and giving a tenth of what we gave back to God anti-dates the law. In Genesis 4, there are some insights into the offerings that Abel brought to the Lord. In this story, Cain and Abel were the first two to bring sacrifices to God. Abel's sacrifice was accepted while Cain's was rejected. We don't know what was all involved in that, but Abel did bring a blood sacrifice. In verse 4, it says that Abel brought *"the firstborn of his flock,"* and that is an interesting thought. So it seems that Abel went out to his flock and gave it to the Lord. He didn't give the left overs or the dregs at the bottom of the cup. He gave the very best. God wants us to bring the best we have, such as, the best quality music, best quality speaking, or even the best of our service. God wants our best! And when it comes to our giving he wants to be number one.

Abel brought God the very first fruits.

The Tithing Principle Presented

Second, in Genesis 14, there is a story of Abraham when Lot was taken captive by wicked kings and they stripped off his possessions. When Abraham heard about it, he pursued those kings and was victorious and brought Lot and the spoil back. On the way back, he encountered a mysterious man by the name of Melchizedeck, who was a Priest. He was an Old Testament type of Christ. Literally his name means *King of Peace*. We read in Genesis 14:

> *Then Melchizedek king of Salem brought out bread and wine. He was priest of God Most High, [19] and he blessed Abram, saying,"Blessed be Abram by God Most High, Creator of heaven and earth.[20] And praise be to God Most High, who delivered your enemies into your hand."Then Abram gave him a tenth of everything.*
> Genesis 14:18-20

I want you to see that this was a principle in the Word of God <u>before</u> Moses even breathed a single breath. This occurred <u>before</u> there was a Law. This was <u>before</u> there was a Mount Sinai.

The principle of tithing was already in the heart of God and being practiced by the Old Testament saints.

Even when you go to the book of Hebrews, the author of Hebrews appeals to this passage and talks about the fact that we who are believers have superseded the Old Covenant with the New Covenant. We, therefore stand on higher ground than Abraham who gave tithes to Melchizedeck in the Old Testament.

At stake is not just a "legalistic" desire by God to pay the bills of Israel or His Church. By placing this principle of "tithing" prior to the "Law" and the first Covenant, God was setting a precedent. He was establishing a priority in the lives of his people. He was trying to teach that his people should put him first, even in their giving.

The Law and Tithing

Moving ahead in biblical history, the Law was established at Mt. Sinai, to Moses, and God spelled it out exactly what the people were to do. I've heard people brag that they are Old Testament "tithers." Well, you better be careful you know what you are saying when you make that statement.

• First, an Old Testament tither was to give the _Lord's Tithe_ and that's recorded for us in Leviticus 27.

A tithe of everything from the land, whether grain from the soil or fruit from the trees, belongs to the Lord; it is holy to the Lord

Leviticus 27:30

• Second, in Deuteronomy 14:22-27, you discover a _Festival Tithe_ for the ceremonial worship of the Lord for all the expenses of worshiping God.

Be sure to set aside a tenth of all that your fields produce each year. [23] *Eat the tithe of your grain, new wine and olive oil, and the firstborn of your herds and flocks in the presence of the Lord your God at the place he will choose as a dwelling for his Name, so that you may learn to revere the Lord your God always.* [24] *But if that place is too distant and you have been blessed by the Lord your God and cannot carry your tithe (because the place where the Lord will choose to put his Name is so far away),* [25] *then exchange your tithe for silver, and take the silver with you and go to the place the Lord your God will choose.* [26] *Use the silver to buy whatever you like: cattle, sheep, wine or other fermented drink, or anything you wish. Then you and your household shall eat there in the presence of the Lord your God and rejoice.*[27] *And do not neglect the Levites living in your towns, for they have no allotment or inheritance of their own.*

Deuteronomy 24:22-27

• Third, every three years they had to give another tithe called the _Poor Tithe._ It's like the benevolent offering that many churches collect to help those who are in need.

When you have finished setting aside a tenth of all your produce in the third year, the year of the tithe, you shall give it to the Levite, the foreigner, the fatherless and the widow, so that they may eat in your towns and be satisfied.

Deuteronomy 26:12

When you add it all up, they were giving 23 1/3% of everything to God. So be careful when you go around bragging that you are an Old Testament tither. Your math better add up!

Should We Be Old Testament Tithers?

Today, our economy is different. The reason we practice the *Lord's Tithe* only is because Israel was a *Nation* and *Religious Institution* all together. When those tithes were collected by Israel - the government agency, military and religious institutions were all combined under one budget. The economy was one and the same.

Today, what we give to God and what we give to the Government, and the military if you are a tither, would total to more than 23%. That is why we only practice the Lord's Tithe because the other offerings are covered under other avenues of giving (taxes) and benevolent offerings.

But how about when you get into the New Testament? Is tithing over when you get there?

The Gospels Teach That Jesus Tithed

Please recognize that the first four gospels fall under the Old Testament because the Holy Spirit did not come until Pentecost, and all of the benefits of the cross were not understood. So then, Matthew, Mark, Luke, and John are technically still under the Old Covenant.

In Matthew 23, Jesus is speaking and he is talking about tithing. Jesus said, *"Woe to you, teachers of the law and Pharisees, you hypocrites! You give a tenth of your spices—mint, dill and cumin. But you have neglected the more important matters of the law—justice, mercy and faithfulness* (Matthew 23:23).

Jesus comes down hard on their hypocrisy, because on the one hand they tithed meticulously, but on the other hand they were nasty people. They were unkind, ungracious, and unloving. Then, after scolding them, Jesus said the following, *"You should have practiced the latter, without neglecting the former.* What was the *former*? Tithing.

Jesus didn't say, *"Stop tithing and only love, love, love."* He said that they needed to do both. I also believed that Jesus fulfilled and tithed everything that he had because the Scriptures said that he fulfilled every aspect of the Law. He didn't come to obliterate the Law. He came to fulfill it.

New Testament and Tithing

Some have observed correctly that you don't have a 10% specific amount set for the New Testament church. But the level of giving is elevated to a higher level above the 10 percentile.

In 1 Corinthians 16 it says, *"On the first day of every week, each one of you should set aside a sum of money in keeping with your income, saving it up, so that when I come no collections will have to be made"* (1 Corinthians 16:1-2).

The key phrase here is *"in keeping with your income."*

This means that you may have to give far more than 10%, because if God has prospered you in amazing ways you could never be satisfied in giving 10%. But tithing is where you start. It is *"God's training wheels"* to generosity.

We want to understand, in later chapters what God desires, but in this chapter my goal has been to show that God instituted the tithe to teach us how to give generously through it. When we are left alone to ourselves we can become rather selfish and even stingy with our resources.

I have found in my life that tithing breaks me out of that selfishness. It is through this disciplined type of giving which allows me to then be open to give in other areas of life.

In our next chapter, we'll look at Malachi 3 and see how Israel struggled with tithing. God was very direct with them about their lack of discipline in this area. Keep reading and understand the importance of generosity and giving.

LIFE APPLICATION

1. What has been your experience with tithing? Did you grow up tithing? Did your family tithe? Was it a negative or positive experience?
2. What do you think about tithing as a way that God teaches us to be generous?
3. What ramifications does it make that tithing was started before the time of the law (Moses) and that it carried through the Gospels?
4. Does it matter that Jesus tithed?

Chapter 5

SIX REASONS TO TITHE

*I*n the Old Testament, whenever they observed the laws, including the principle of tithing, the nation of Israel was blessed by God. Whenever they put these laws aside, God judged them. In fact, there was a period of time when they fell away from these laws, and under the leadership of Malachi they were challenged to come back.

In Malachi chapter 3, the nation of Israel had forsaken this standard, and Malachi pleads with them to come back to God's standard. They had stopped tithing and Malachi, who is a powerful confrontational type of prophet, gets right to the point and says in verse 10:

"Bring the whole tithe into the storehouse, that there may

*be food in my house. Test me in this," says
the Lord Almighty,"and see if I will not throw open the
floodgates of heaven and pour out so much blessing that
there will not be room enough to store it"*

Malachi 3:10

Six Reasons Why Tithing Is Important

In this passage, there are six reasons we want to see why this is important to you and me.

1. We Make God First Place In Our Lives.

First, when we tithe we put God first. If you read in Malachi, you'll discover that some of the people had started to do things that they shouldn't have done. They were giving to God, but not really tithing to God. It is possible that some of you reading this book can be giving to the Lord's work, but not putting God first in your giving. There is a vast difference.

Malachi 1:8 says, *"When you offer blind animals for sacrifice, is that not wrong? When you sacrifice lame or diseased animals, is that not wrong? Try offering them to your governor! Would he be pleased with you? Would he accept you?" says the Lord Almighty.*

Then in verse 14 it says,

"Cursed is the cheat who has an acceptable male in his flock and vows to give it, but then sacrifices a blemished animal to the Lord. For I am a great king," says the Lord Almighty, "and my name is to be feared among the nations"

Malachi 1:14

*W*hat they were doing was giving "the sorriest creature" that they could find from their flocks, giving it to God and calling it a "tithe." They would pick out a "blind, diseased or lame animal" and give it to God. I think the principle that needs to be emphasized is to give God the *first fruits*. In our family, I try to make sure that our tithe is always first provided. These days, most churches have some sort of giving Mobile Application on their website or phone (APP) where a member can give online. I think that this is one of the greatest tools to make sure that God always gets the tithe first.

Is it always important that you "just get it done?" No! Of course, your heart and attitude need to be properly attached. But it is an act of worship that says that every time you do it, God should take priority in your life.

2. We Demonstrate God Is True To His Word.

A second reason tithing is important is that we demonstrate God can be trusted. In verse 10, we read,

> *"Bring the whole tithe into the storehouse, that there may*
> *be food in my house. Test me in this," says*
> *the Lord Almighty..."* (Malachi 3:10a).

Literally, the word *test* means "to prove." Everybody wants to know whether they can afford to tithe or not. People have said to me, "Pastor, you don't know how many bills I have." My response has always been to say, "The best thing that you can do is to give to God your first priority because you will then see how God will take care of the rest of your life."

If you say, "I'm going to wait until I get it all straightened out, then I'll start giving to God," what are you doing? You are putting God at the bottom of the priority list! You are saying to God, "When I get things straightened out in my life that's when I'll start to give." But the probability of that happening is very low.

Putting God first helps you get other things in order. The Bible is saying here, "When you tithe, test God! Put God to a test!"

I've heard people say that it's easier to live on 90%

when you start giving God the first 10%, than when you were living on 100%. I'm not saying that it's going to be a cakewalk. It is going to require some discipline in your finances, but what I am saying is that if God says that he is going to bless us, then he will.

I can testify that when you practice tithing God will never sell you short. My challenge to you is to test God! I challenge you to start right now and tithe and see how God will bless you in ways you never dreamed.

In fact, there are four types of blessings God will give you as you practice the principle of tithing.

The Blessings

In verse 11, it says,

> *I will prevent pests from devouring your crops, and the vines in your fields will not drop their fruit before it is ripe, says the Lord Almighty.* [12] *"Then all the nations will call you blessed, for yours will be a delightful land," says the Lord Almighty.*
> Malachi 3:11-12

Notice, that this is not a pastor promising you this!

This is not some financial economist promising you this! This is God promising you four very specific blessings.

Personal Blessing

First, He will provide a personal blessing. In verse 10, He says, *"and see if I will not throw open the floodgates of heaven and pour out so much blessing that there will not be room enough to store it."* Does God still do this? Yes He does! He sends blessings from places and ways that you never dreamed of. God provides for your needs. He cares for the things going on in your life. I am telling you that no matter how much money you have or how long it has been since you have given it to God, you cannot out-give God. For when you begin to give to God what he has entrusted to you, in the way that he wants you to give, you can expect God to do things in your life that you never expected.

Material Blessing

Second, He will provide a material blessing. He says in verse 10 that he will pour out so much that we will not have room to contain it. Proverbs 3:9-10 says it this way, *"Honor the Lord with your wealth, with the first fruits of all your crops; [10] then your barns will be filled to overflowing, and your vats will brim over with new wine."*

Economic Blessing

Third, He will rebuke the pests that devour your incomes. In that Old Testament economy, it meant that they didn't get blight in their vines, and their crops didn't fail. But how does God *"rebuke the pests that devour"* in our day? There are so many ways that He does that! The "pests that devour" is Satan. First Peter 5: 8 says, *Be alert and of sober mind. Your enemy the devil prowls around like a roaring lion looking for someone to devour.* God has already said that he will rebuke the "devour" on our behalf if we choose to trust in him. I think of two ways that God provides for me on a daily basis. Either he gives me more money or he keeps my bills down (the pests). Either way, it's a win-win for you and me!

Spiritual Blessing

Fourth, He will give a spiritual blessing. In verse 12, it says, *"Then all the nations will call you blessed, for yours will be a delightful land," says the Lord Almighty.* It's just another way of saying that God will honor you and your people. I like to think that God honors a Church who believes in tithing.

3. We Honor The Lord's Name To The Nations.

A third reason tithing is important is because of our

testimony to the nations. In Malachi 3:12, it says, *"Then all the nations will call you blessed, for yours will be a delightful land, says the LORD Almighty."* Proverbs 3:9 says, *"Honor the Lord with your wealth, with the first fruits of all your crops."*

These verses are saying that when we give to God, we are honoring the Lord's name. I think especially of George Mueller who started an orphanage in England. It was once estimated that he gave away 86% of his personal donations. He could have lived lavishly, but he chose to live modestly to the end of his life. He once said, *"My aim was never how much I could obtain, but how much I could give."* Because of his work, thousands of children were given a home to live here on earth and a heavenly home through Jesus Christ!

Do you look at your money in that way? Do you look at your offerings in that fashion? Do you see your income as a conduit to reaching the world for Christ?

4. It Makes God Real To Us.

A fourth reason tithing is important is that it makes God real to us. If you go through the Old Testament one thing that you will find about giving is that God takes "gifts and giving" in a very personal way. God personally gets involved with us when we give. And he personally holds us accountable for what we give. I'm sure that God someday may read our church Annual Report. But it seems that God is much more interested in our individual giving patterns because, when we come to the New Testament passages on stewardship, they seem to emphasize the individual and not corporate patterns. Notice the passages below:

"On the first day of every week, each one of you should set aside a sum of money in keeping with your income, saving it up, so that when I come no collections will have to be made." That means that our gifts are judged individually, not corporately as a church.
1 Corinthians 16:2

Nevertheless, the one who receives instruction in the word should share all good things with their instructor.
Galatians 6:6

Now about the collection for the Lord's people: Do what I told the Galatian churches to do. [2] On the first day of every week, each one of you should set aside a sum of money in keeping with your income, saving it up, so that when I come no collections will have to be made. [3] Then, when I arrive, I will give letters of introduction to the men you approve and send them with your gift to

Jerusalem. ⁴ If it seems advisable for me to go also, they
will accompany me.
1 Corinthians 16:1-2

My point is that God in His Word is emphasizing the *individual* giving, rather than the *corporate* giving in our church. And so, if you think that you can look at the "bottom line" of the ministry and say, "well, the church doesn't need it" and forsake your gift, then you are fooling only yourself. Your personal giving is one that the Lord is greatly interested in. God looks into our own lives and examines us.

The Bible does say that that all of us, as Christians, will one day give an account. For God does keep track of what we do. That's not a scare tactic, that's just the truth! I don't know if God has a ledger in Heaven. I just know that God is personally involved when we give to him.

And if you want to have a personal involvement with God, just get involved with him and do what he says. For happy is the person who learns early to obey Almighty God.

5. We Practice Godliness.

A fifth reason why we tithe centers on godliness. The question that some are asking at this point is *"am I going to be a better Christian if I tithe?"* The only way to answer that question is to say that if you don't do something that God tells you to do then you are being <u>disobedient</u>. This is probably the hardest thing that I can write in this book that will offend some of you who have been Christians a long time but have not believed in tithing.

It's like when I speak to Christians who have been Christians for a long time and they have never been "baptized by immersion" and I share with them that they need to be in order to be obedient to God's Word. They look at me as if I am "looking down my nose at them." No! I'm just trying to help them realize that they are disobedient and I want to them to be obedient to Christ's command.

I look at this way. There are a lot of things which are left up to our own decisions when it comes to church polity and practice. We can have church services on Saturday or Sunday. We can have various styles of music. I, as a pastor, can preach in a suit or in jeans. But when it comes to "tithing" I know exactly what God wants me to do and he wants me to give.

And for me, it is the starting block. It is the "training wheels" to learning how to give generously. It is how God begins to release me from my selfishness.

And so, if you want to be a godly person, then you need to start obeying God's Word, and this is one of those areas. For godliness is obedience where we do not argue with him. We just do it!

Let me tell you something about obedience. When you begin to obey God, there is a greater sense of joy in your life because you are measuring your life not against your own attributes, but you've measured your life against God's will. That is a real measure of godliness.

If you want to get down to the real source of godliness, it's not really about the words that you say, but it's about the life that you live. You can get into a lot of difficult questions and rationale when it comes to this subject, but it really comes down to a very basic question of "obedience" and what we are going to do with what God has said.

6. We Participate In God's Work.

Lastly, we participate in God's work when we tithe. In Malachi 3, it says, " *Bring the whole tithe into the* <u>*storehouse*</u>." I must inform you that there is a big argument out in the Christian community concerning *storehouse giving*. But whatever you get out of this passage don't miss the sense of community. They are not using their <u>own gifts</u>, but they are bringing their own gifts for the benefit of the total group. So that together, their gifts make a difference.

When it comes to supporting a church or any ministry, not one person can do it alone, regardless how much money that person has. The thought here is that what we can't do by ourselves, we can do together. And when we put our resources together we get a sense that we are participating in something far bigger than ourselves.

When we tithe, we participate in the ministry of God's work.

Concluding Thoughts

What it comes down to is that when you tithe you know that you are doing the right thing. You realize that you are putting God first. You know that you are following God obediently. You know that you have joined with God's people to produce spiritual results. You start to listen to missionary reports because you have an investment in it. You begin to care about what is going on in the children's ministry department because you are making that possible. You start to pray for the youth retreats when they are mentioned from the pulpit.

When you begin to tithe, you move from the

perimeter of the circle to the center of it. Again, tithing is not some legalistic, rule oriented mechanism designed by God to pay the bills. If you have that impression then you are completely wrong. God designed it as a means of teaching his people generosity. It is a tool to help us understand community and what it really means to take care of one another.

If you are not tithing, then take the step this year. Do it by faith. Don't do it because this book is telling you to do it or this pastor is telling you to do it.

Do it because God's Word teaches it and you know that if you follow God's Word he will bless you.

LIFE APPLICATION

1. Which is the hardest part of tithing to you? Is it trusting God with your money, or simply a lack of desire to give? Or is it another reason?
2. Do you agree that the tithing is the beginning place to generosity? How does our willingness to pay tithes and offerings show gratitude to our Heavenly Father for all His blessings to us?
3. With all the benefits to tithing what would be the negatives to it? Try to give Biblical credence to your reasons.

Chapter 6

THE FEAR OF GIVING
TOO MUCH

*T*he Stolzfus family had moved from Ohio to a farm in Pennsylvania for a promise of wonderful crops and endless fields of corn. And for a while, that's exactly what they found. And throughout the 1940's, found their way to Pennsylvania, started farms and found prosperity. Then a drought occurred, where under the baking sun, the land was devastated. It seemed that the drought would never end.

To make matters worse, the wind whipped up storms in a moments notice which produced momentary showers, but nothing with any substance. This was so overwhelming to James Stoltzfus because every-time he sowed his fields, he would spend a month's salary on his seeds. After three years with little or no income it was getting to the point where he couldn't afford to keep up the routine much longer. Like many of the farmers in his shoes, James had sleepless nights. During the normal growing seasons, he would stockpile the seeds, but under the strain of the drought seasons, he would fall into the worry:

What if another wind storm comes and blows away my investment? What if all my efforts get wiped away again? What if...what if...what if...

James began to get a strange attachment to his seeds. He knew that they were worthless sitting in the barn, but he couldn't help feeling that it was better off keeping them there until he knew his chances would be better to get a greater crop.

After a while, many of the farmers began to plant their seeds. It was spring and the days of germination would end soon and another hot summer wound begin. So, If he didn't plant soon, he'd miss yet another chance. Daily he would go to the barn and look at the seeds and pace back and forth thinking, "Should I or shouldn't I?" It was almost overwhelming to him.

James wasn't a greedy man. But the weight of uncertainty was making him almost irrational about his seeds.

What If I Give Away Too Much

Think about it. You and I are much like James. Every day, we brace for ruin that can sweep our financial life and wipe out our puny little seeds. We live with the "what if's" that diminish our retirement accounts, savings and unexpected expenses. We hope for the best.

In the midst of it all, we have a crop to produce – a spiritual crop. Like James, we have a limited supply of seed for sowing in God's kingdom. Perhaps you once dreamed of sowing fertile fields of generosity. But reality has taught you to be more cautious.

What if I give away too much?
What if there's not enough left for me?
What if… What if…What if…

We are not greedy, but we are a lot like James. Under the mounting pressure of uncertainty, it's easy to become irrational about our possessions. We lose sight of who owns them. We fail to grasp how we should be sowing them for God's kingdom. We get confused about what we should really fear regarding our finances in this life – like facing eternity having sown only a few handfuls of our personal wealth for God's kingdom.

We're not alone. There are a lot of people in the world just like us who feel that same type of anxiety. In all likelihood, they want to be generous. They want to tithe. But somewhere along the way, uncertainty creeps in and they settle for the status quo. They settle for a watered down version of what they could be sowing for God's kingdom – if it weren't for their fears.

According to the *Christian Research Institute*, in the United States only one-third to one half give any financial support to their church.

But out of those who do give, only 3-5% actually tithe to their church.

Meanwhile, the wealth accumulated by churchgoing people has reached record levels. And despite opportunities for global ministry, American Christians give proportionately less today to the church than they did during the Great Depression.

I think that the problem is not brand awareness, nor is it that Christians are greedy and miserly people. But I believe, that for most people, the lack of generosity can be attributed to fear.

Jesus Address This Fear

Fear has always been one of the principle enemies of a growing faith. It has always clouded our thinking and obscured our path. When it comes to how we spend our money it really does affect us. It's important to realize that fear and faith go together. By nature, if you want to pursue a growing faith then your fears need to diminish.

Many Christians realize how much they would love to give to the Lord's work, but fear kicks in before they can bridge the gap with faith. It is no accident that the Lord addresses this condition head-on. In Matthew 6:33, he says, *"But seek first his kingdom and his righteousness, and all these things will be given to you as well."* Jesus is saying that when we seek his Kingdom, we don't have to fear being wiped out for he will give you all you need from day to day if you live for him, and make the kingdom of God your primary concern.

We are about to discover in the next few chapters how to dismantle our fears and begin to live by faith. Because it is only as we begin to live by faith that generosity, giving and tithing all makes sense.

LIFE APPLICATION

1. Is the core issue of why you don't tithe or give a percentage of your income to the Lord's work come out of "fear"?
2. Do you see the battle between fear and faith in the area of generosity? What if I give away too much? What if…?
3. How do you battle this tug of war in your heart when it comes to giving and generosity?

Chapter 7

DISMANTLING OUR FEAR

*M*ost people have probably heard the name R.G. LeTourneau. Mr. LeTourneau was the designer and manufacturer of heavy earth moving equipment. His equipment is what transformed the five-thousand acres of marsh land into New York's Kennedy Airport. It was his equipment that made it possible for the fighters to land on the beaches of Ormandy on D-Day. LeTourneau is the recognized leader in large earth moving machines.

In the early years, LeTourneau went into a partnership with God. Because he believed that God owned it all, he dedicated his factory to the Lord. So in 1935, he irrevocably assigned 90% of the profits to the LeTourneau Foundation, which could only be used for the cause of Christ.

In the first five years of its existence, the foundation gave over five million dollars to the work of Jesus Christ around the world. R.G. LeTourneau's attitude towards money is expressed in the book, *The Man who Moved Men and Mountains*. Nels Stelstrom, the Assistant President of LeTourneau College, wrote the Epilogue to the book and he said this:

R.G. does not view money as something to be accumulated or as something for the satisfaction of looking at it, or counting it each day to see its increase, or the measure of a man's worth. He sees it as a means to produce a machine his mind has conceived or as a means to bring men to God. Although he made and spent millions, he was remarkably detracted from money. He only had one concern and that was, what can that money accomplish? He often said, "It's not how much money I give to God, but rather how much of God's money I keep for myself."

Finding Your Giving Threshold

LeTourneau's story has a way of putting things in perspective. It should make us think twice before we throw out words like generosity and self-sacrifice. Some consider him extreme, but he certainly took giving seriously.

Before we go any further, let's get a little more personal.

When you read LeTourneau's story how did you feel about your own giving? Did you feel challenged? Convicted? Depressed? Would you consider giving away 90% of your income for God's kingdom work?

Okay, maybe that's a little too high. So let's go a little lower?

• 50%?

• 40%?

• 30% sound reasonable?

• How about 20%?

• Or even 10%?

I have a confession to make. My entire purpose in telling the story was to test you. For most of us, the idea of giving away huge amounts of money elicits a sense of fear. When challenged to give away more, what kinds of feelings did you experience? Maybe it caused you to entertain some ways to increase your giving by making sacrifices or possibly making lifestyle changes.

Here's a scary thought: *What if God called you to give*

beyond your comfort level? Would you be afraid? Would you try to explain it away or dismiss it as impractical? You see, when we respond in fear to an invitation from God, we forfeit the reward of an invitation for being faithful stewards.

Remember James Stolzfus? Sowing in faith results in eternal crops. Trembling in fear yields to empty fields.

When we hear stories like LeTourneau, and others like him, there is a tendency to begin to become numb to them. We discount their stories as unattainable and impossible extremes. We toss them into a category as Mother Theresa and countless other examples of people that we cannot measure up. We admire them as remarkable people, but certainly do not follow their lead.

Think again about your fear of how giving more made you feel.

• Were you uncomfortable?

• Were you afraid?

• What kind of thoughts went through your mind as I challenged you with percentages?

• Did you start to list the reasons why you can't give beyond a certain point?

• Did any "what ifs…" come to mind?

Everyone has a threshold when it comes to giving. Whether it's a dollar amount or a percentage. No matter how far you are willing to go for God's kingdom, sooner or later you are going to hit the wall.

For many Christians, the wall is fear. Until you recognize it, you'll never be able to break through it.

Dismantling The Fear of Giving

In the giving community there are two types of givers. First, there are those who give what is left over and there are those who give off the top.

The first group who gives off what is left over isn't greedy. They just see that they are responsible for meeting their own needs first. And then, whatever is left goes to the Lord's work.

The second group sees everything as belonging to God including the responsibility to meet their daily needs. Therefore, they're free to take on the mission of stewarding God's resources as their generosity dictates. Generosity is their priority.

The problem with giving leftovers is that your generosity can never exceed your ability to meet your needs. If you prosper, there may be some left over. But the minute you face financial uncertainty, generosity takes a backseat. In 2 Corinthians 9:7, the apostle Paul says, *"Each of you should give what you have decided in your heart to give, not reluctantly or under compulsion, for God loves a cheerful giver."* But the more your heart is occupied with the burden of meeting your needs, the less it can entertain God's prompting to be generous.

For the people in the second group, the generous givers, giving off the top is only logical. They understand that God owns and controls it all. They feel free to invest in his interests first and their own needs second. It's the rational thing to do.

For leftover givers, it's always a struggle to let go in this area. They've heard the sermons. They heard pleas. But they have families to feed and retirements to fund. So they hold back on God, afraid they can't manage all their financial responsibilities. Isn't it more rational to give off the top and trust God with your finances since it all belongs to him? And isn't it rational to trust God with something that is beyond your control anyway?

Fear has a way of twisting the truth.

Beyond My Comfort Zone

As you grow in your relationship with the Lord, occasionally God will test your grip on your wallet. It's a faith issue. It doesn't happen every month, but it does happen occasionally. God will prompt you to step out of your comfort zone. And if you really want to follow God, then you will have to trust him by not stockpiling.

I'm not talking about acting irresponsibly with your money. I'm talking about the clear voice of God when he speaks to give to the needs of his kingdom work.

For example, ten percent, for the most part, has been pretty easy for me. I was taught to give a tithe from my first allowance as a child from my parents. For both my wife and me, tithing is well within our comfort zone. I could tithe my entire life without getting close to the fear threshold. But throughout my life, there have been moments when I was challenged to go beyond my regular giving and each time, I must confess I faced fear.

Fear is a regular part of the landscape of anyone who wants to grow in faith. I remember the first time. There was a famine in India, and I was in High

School. My Sunday School teacher presented the need about the children who needed money for food and water. I was already tithing from working in a machine shop cleaning machines trying to earn some money for a car. The idea of giving above my tithe to this cause was monumental. On the one hand, I wanted to be generous. On the other hand, I was afraid of what it would do to my budget. In the end, I gave the money. The fear never went away, but for whatever reason I resolved to give to the Lord's work beyond my tithe. I'm not sure what difference that money made all the way in India. But I do know that it made a huge difference in my life. It was a defining moment because if you get prompted to give beyond your regular giving (through the work of the Holy Spirit) enough times, your level of generosity will naturally grow. I know that it did so in my life!

Key Issue

The solution to the tension between obedience and fear lies with our idea of ownership.

Who really is the owner of your possessions? And who's calling the shots for you financially? If you believe everything truly belongs to God, then you have nothing to fear after all.

And if God is the source of wealth and he controls the comings and goings of your money, then there's no reason not to give.

In every person's life, God plants the question: "Do you trust me?" To trust in him financially means we experience peace and contentment while we enjoy the thrill of participating in his financial mission for the world.

Maybe God isn't calling you to give at the level of LeTourneau. But has he ever prompted you to a level of generosity that felt a little uncomfortable?

Has fear ever kept you from following Him and doing something financially daring for His kingdom? Is it possible that you could get to the end of your life and never know for sure?

Spend time praying over where the line is for you. But if you really want to move beyond your fear, to experience the joy of generosity, then brace yourself for a life changing principle.

LIFE APPLICATION

1. What's your giving threshold? Is it 1%, 5%, 10%, 20%? What is it?
2. At what percentage of giving starts to make you uncomfortable when it comes to generosity and giving to the Lord's work?
3. Do you see that faith is the issue when it comes to stretching your comfort zone in giving?

Chapter 8

THE PLAN TAKES SHAPE

*I*t's very clear that God loves and wants a cheerful giver to be the backbone of his generosity plan. But let's face it: relying on waves of generosity isn't much of a plan by itself. So let's go a step further and give some structure to generosity. Hopefully these guidelines will help you as we conclude this book.

Of course, this isn't a black-and-white, step-by-step sort of thing. Moreover it is a blueprint that will keep you in sync with God's heart on giving. I don't think it's enough to only give "as the Spirit leads," that is, whenever the idea hits you. Sure, God will give you spontaneous ideas from time to time, and generosity should always be your overriding motive. But the idea of planning is central to what the Bible says about finances. Besides, giving without a plan makes you vulnerable to your own emotions, and emotions can make you influenced by fear.

So the best strategy is to give strategically. Here are four insights.

Priority Giving

Of all the items in your monthly budget, giving should be the top priority. It should not just be *a* priority, but the first one. In other words, before you pay your mortgage, or buy groceries, or pay any other bill. The very first check you need to write is to your local church.

Here's why: If you wait until other expenses are met first, it will impact the bottom line of your giving. That's just the way it works with priorities. Whatever is first place will take precedence over everything else. In fact, God means for it to be the primary impetus behind your giving plan. Waiting until that provision has dwindled and been reduced by your monthly obligations has a tendency to squelch generosity. However, if you prioritize your giving, then everything else will take its proper place in line behind the priority of God's work.

By prioritizing God in your checkbook ledger, you avoid running short when it comes time to give him his share. Imagine having God at a dinner party, but serving him last and running out of food! Ooops! So you go to the refrigerator and scrape him up some leftovers. I'm sure that would never happen in your home. He would get the best seat and the best food. We would honor him with priority. Yet, we do that with our finances. Determine to give him priority in your giving.

Percentage Giving

The second principle that we want to stress in this book is percentage giving. What I like most about percentage giving is that it objectifies the entire giving process. Remember that the more you can do to keep fear from influencing your wallet, the less you risk drifting away from God in your finances. When you commit to give a percentage of your income to God, it's pretty clear cut and dry. The numbers don't lie. Ten percent is ten percent whether you feel confident that your heavenly Father will provide your needs or not. So whatever percentage you choose, you have a target you can aim for no matter how much your emotions fluctuate.

Let me shed some light on tithing. I've talked a little about it in this book, and some of you may be convinced of this percentage and some may not. But that's not necessary.

Picture yourself receiving ten one dollar bills from God. Remember, God is the owner and you're just a steward and not the owner. As you look at the bills in your hand, you say, "God, you're handing me ten of your dollars. What do you want me to do with them? Are you going to want them back?"

God just says, "I just want one of them back." Puzzled, you reply, "Just one? Are you sure?" "Yes," he says.

"Well, what do you want me to do with the other nine?" you respond.

"Whatever you want," he says.

In disbelief you say, "So I can keep all nine of these and you only want one back?"

"Yes," he says.

Now, you get the idea. It's almost ridiculous. If you truly saw your income as his, then giving him a percentage of your income would be more than appropriate. And if you are searching the Bible for a percentage, then 10% is a good place to start. It was the amount God used to start teaching his people how to give. I'm not sure why God chose 10%, but he did. And I believe that 10% is a good starting point for us today.

So are you willing to try 10% or is that a little too scary for you?

Whether you are ready to tithe or not, I want to encourage you to pick a percentage number and begin giving. It's the best way to create a benchmark and get a handle on an otherwise intangible decision-making process.

What percentage can you see yourself giving? How about 5%? Even if your knees are quivering and you can only muster up 1%, I urge you to commit to something and stick to it. Try it for a period of time; raise that percentage and see how God provides for you. You won't even notice the monies missing.

It's important to start somewhere – anywhere. Because until you try, you won't put yourself in a position to experience the intervention of the Creator of all economy as he begins to move in the area of your finances. Once you encounter him firsthand, your motivation will skyrocket. *So pick your percentage and start with your next paycheck.*

Proportional Giving

The third principle that comes from this book is the principle of proportional giving. Proportional giving occurs when you increase your percentage giving over the years. If you've been giving 10 percent for several years, maybe it is time to move up to 12 percent or 15 percent. Another way to say this principle is "progressive." We increase our giving as we progress through life.

Here's why I think it's a good idea. Your faith and your faithfulness grow hand in hand. You can't separate them. And if your faith is to thrive and grow, your faithfulness must also develop.

As long as you are alive on this earth, God intends for your faith to be growing. His agenda for your life is that you be gradually transformed, little by little, to the likeness of Christ. That's the nature of faith. Its progress is steady, and its target is Christ-likeness. Now, when it comes to your finances, you need to be growing in faith there as well. But you can't grow as a giver if you don't also increase your giving. In other words, if you've been tithing for twenty years and you've never increased your percentage of giving, you haven't grown. Sure, you've been faithful in terms of steadfastness. And that's great. But in order for your faith to grow, it needs to be stretched from time to time. And that means progressively increasing the percentage you entrust to God as the owner of your finances.

Over the years, Beth and I have been challenged to bump up our giving on several occasions. It's not every year, but we can usually tell when it's time to rethink our goals. When you first start tithing it is such a spiritual experience. You can hardly believe you are voluntarily doing something in the face of normal economics. That you are trusting God for your future! But after a while, it's easy to tithe. It does become second nature.

That's why a growing faith is all about proportional giving over the long haul.

Prompted Giving

One last area of giving that I want to encourage you is prompted giving. Having a plan is important, but from time to time, God may prompt you to make a special gift that goes beyond a rote formula. For instance, As a lead pastor, I rarely have the opportunity to sit and listen to a speaker, but one Sunday at our church, nationally known Youth Speaker, Bob Lenz was speaking, and at the end of the service he made an appeal to come back and speak at the local high school. God really tugged at my heart, as he did others that day, to give a love gift toward this need. I looked at my wife and we were both in agreement that we should give something. This is what I mean by prompted giving. It wasn't a part of our regular giving. It was over and above our regular tithe.

Prompted giving is sacrificial. Prompted giving changes your perspective. You no longer view God as a vending machine. Instead, you begin to see Him as your personal heavenly Father who is at work in the world and wants you to be a part of that work.

In 1 John 3:17, Jesus asks, *"If anyone has material possessions and sees a brother or sister in need but has no pity on them, how can the love of God be in that person?"* God uses the needs of others as opportunities for us to exhibit his love alive in us. And many of those opportunities are revealed through special promptings that are above and beyond our regular and scheduled giving.

LIFE APPLICATION

1. Are you willing to try 10% or is that too scary? OK, then pick a number and begin a percentage giving. It's the best way to create benchmarks and get a handle on an otherwise intangible decision-making process. How about 5%? Or Just 1 %?

2. If you do tithe (10%) have you begun to give *in proportion to your income* as God has blessed you? Maybe you need to stretch yourself and go beyond your fear into faith?

3. Maybe you need to start to pray about your giving habits? Are there changes that need to be made in your life?

Chapter 9

THE TARGET OF GENEROSITY

*I*f you're like me then you're wondering how to reflect on this idea of giving and generosity.

How do I measure up?

Where do I go from where I am to where God wants me to go?

We've already talked about priority, percentages, proportional, and prompted giving. But I don't want you to get distracted from the whole point of the book which is generosity. You see, those four "P's" are strong guidelines to follow. But the ultimate reward when we move in God's direction is to experience the joy of giving.

If I could give you the target to shoot for, that would

be it. Like I've suggested at the start, it's not so much about percentages or dollar amounts.

It's not about legalism.

It's more about the condition of the heart. It's about a joyful heart.

There's no better way to measure it. You'll know when you've gotten beyond your fear when you begin to experience joy in the act of giving. It may not happen instantly. It may come so gradually that you hardly notice it. But little by little, you'll know you've arrived when the thrill of making a financial impact begins to consume and fill you with joy.

All around the world there are people who are motivated to give to fulfill the commands of Scripture. That's a start. The goal is to discover the joy of living in an intimate financial partnership with our heavenly Father. And when we do, giving becomes an exciting, passion-filled act of worship.

But as some point, giving must move from the "have to" column to the "want to" column of our lives. That will not happen until we wrestle our fears to the ground and learn to trust in God. Trust is a great concept.

So I want to ask you a concluding question: Is giving

a passionate pursuit in your life? Does it feel like an act of worship? Does it bring you joy? The way you answer those questions will be an indication of where you are in your journey from fear to joy. The way you answer those questions will be an indication of where you are from self-dependence to trusting in God for your daily provision. If you're anything less than thrilled about giving generously, then you still have a way to go.

The Manager Story

Bill Cramer who was an assistant manager in a large manufacturing company. He was a hard working employee laboring for sixty hours a week on average. As a twenty-five year employee, Bill was the backbone of his company. One day, Bill received a phone call that a rich uncle of his had died and left him a large sum of money, but the estate had some unusual terms. Uncle Mike had set up a foundation for his remaining assets and wanted his nephew to distribute nearly one million dollars, but he had to do it within twelve years. Consequently, Bill began to distribute the monies to various needful organizations.

In the months to follow, Bill began to receive reports on the work that various organizations had accomplished. He saw how starving people were fed and abandoned children could receive medical treatment. He learned about itinerant farmers and new cultivating processes in foreign villages. At first, Bill showed little interest. Eventually, his outer tough shell was softened and he felt a sense of urgency.

Bill began to reallocate the foundation's funds to some of these organizations. He then began to make annual treks to see them first hand. He was captivated.

Before long, he decided to take some time off from the plant in order to spend his summers as a volunteer relief worker. Soon after, Bill became involved in a third world relief agency with agricultural training.

Eventually, his Uncle's money dried up four years ahead of schedule. And when that happened, he did the unthinkable: He transferred his own nest egg over to the foundation. Bill continued to work for nine months at the plant and three months at his new calling. He finally retired from the plant at seventy one years old and remained connected to the foundation for another fifteen years until his death.

There was no fear in Bill's quest to give away his uncle's fortune because it was not his money. Bill wasn't worried about how it would affect his life and without the affect of fear in the equation, Bill quickly became seduced by something we were created to experience – the joy of giving.

What if it were you?

Imagine for a minute that you are responsible for giving away someone else's money. You aren't allowed to spend it. You can only decide where it goes. When you think of it that way, it's not too hard to imagine finding pleasure in playing the great philanthropist.

Who wouldn't enjoy being the lifeline to those who need it? What man or woman wouldn't sleep a little better knowing he or she had made a difference in the world?

And yet, when we have a proper perspective on our possessions, that's exactly the situation we find ourselves in. We have been given someone else's money. We have been given the opportunity to decide where it goes.

Are You A Reluctant Giver?

Maybe you are a reluctant giver. I'd like to encourage you with this thought: Just beyond the fear that is dulling your generosity awaits a great amount of joy.

A farmer doesn't obtain seed to consume it or to stockpile it. He only decides to plant it. And only when the seed has been permanently cast into the ground is a harvest returned. That's how joy is received. That's how true significance is gained.

If fear is keeping you from doing a good thing, then you may be missing out on a blessing. In the end, you may be missing out on so much joy! Don't be a reluctant giver. Give generously!